P9-ELQ-447

Political & Economic Systems

COMMUNISM

David Downing

Heinemann Library
Chicago, Illinois

CABARRUS COUNTY PUBLIC LIBRARY
KANNAPOLIS LIBRARY
KANNAPOLIS, NORTH CAROLINA 28081

3 3083 00418 3668

2003 Reed Educational & Professional Publishing
Published by Heinemann Library,
an imprint of Reed Educational and Professional Publishing,
Chicago, Illinois

Customer Service 888–454–2279

Visit our website at www.heinemannlibrary.com

All rights reserved. No part of this publication may be reproduced or transmitted in any form or by any means, electronic or mechanical, including photocopying, recording, taping, or any information storage and retrieval system, without permission in writing from the publisher.

Designed by AMR
Illustrated by Art Construction
Originated by Dot Gradations
Printed in Hong Kong by South China Printing

07 06 05 04 03
10 9 8 7 6 5 4 3 2

Library of Congress Cataloging-in-Publication Data

Downing, David, 1946 Aug. 9-
Communism / David Downing.
p. cm. -- (Political and economic systems)
Includes bibliographical references and index.
ISBN 1-40340-316-3
1. Communism--Juvenile literature. [1. Communism.] I. Title. II. Series.
HX21 .D693 2003
335.43--dc21
2002006317

Acknowledgements
The publishers would like to thank the following for permission to reproduce photographs: Popperfoto/Michael Probst Reuters, p. 4; Hulton Archive, pp. 7, 9, 13, 27, 22, 39, 41, 43; Novosti, pp. 10, 19; Slava Katamidze Collection/Hulton Archive, p. 16; Corbis/Bettmann, pp. 17, 32, 46; Popperfoto, pp. 23, 28, 44, 53; David King Collection, pp. 24, 33; Rex/Rob Steerwood, p. 30; Popperfoto/Darren Whiteside Reuters, p. 35; Popperfoto/Reuter/Bettmann, p. 36; Corbis/Hulton-Deutsch Collection, p. 37; Popperfoto/Vitaly Armand, p. 47; Popperfoto/Alexander Natruskin Reuters, p. 48; Popperfoto/Jamil Bittar Reuters, p. 50; Corbis/David and Peter Turnley, p. 55.

Cover photograph: Chinese children chanting from *The Little Red Book* of Mao Zedong, reproduced with permission of Camera Press.

Every effort has been made to contact copyright holders of any material reproduced in this book. Any omissions will be rectified in subsequent printings if notice is given to the publishers.

Our thanks to Christopher Gibb for his comments in the preparation of this book.

Disclaimer
All the Internet addresses (URLs) given in this book were valid at the time of going to press. However, due to the dynamic nature of the Internet, some addresses may have changed, or sites may have ceased to exist since publication. While the author and publishers regret any inconvenience this may cause readers, no responsibility for any such changes can be accepted by either the author or the publishers.

Some words are shown in bold, **like this.** You can find out what they mean by looking in the glossary.

Contents

1. Two Walls 4

2. Ideas and Ideals 6

3. Taking Power 11

4. Keeping Power 17

5. The One-Party State 21

6. The Planned Economy 26

7. The Totalitarian Society 31

8. Foreign Relations 37

9. Inflexibility and Collapse 42

10. Communism in the 21st Century 48

11. So, What Is Communism? 52

Timeline 56

Sources for Further Research 58

Key Figures in the History of Communism 59

Glossary 61

Index 64

BEST BOOKS 19.95 (15.96) 1-15-04 KA

1 Two Walls

In November 1989, amidst scenes of great joy and excitement, the high and heavily fortified wall that divided the communist and western halves of Berlin was torn down by the people of that city. Since it was built in 1961, the Berlin Wall had offered stark proof of the brutality of **communism.** It was a prison wall, built to prevent people from leaving communist East Germany for the freedom and opportunity found in the West. Nearly 100 people had been shot dead trying to escape through its tangles of barbed wire.

A German youth uses a hammer and chisel to collect a souvenir of the Berlin Wall, several months after its fall in November of 1989.

The wall had divided Berlin, but it had also symbolized the division of the whole world into communist and **capitalist** blocs, or areas. The destruction of the wall in 1989 marked the end of European communism as a global power, the end of a 70-year experiment that had clearly failed.

Seven hundred miles to the east, in Moscow, another long wall surrounded the centuries-old fortress of the Russian Kremlin, which for all of those 70 years had been the nerve center of world communism. The graves of ex-communists killed in the early years of the 1917 **October Revolution** were located along the stretch of wall facing the Red Square. A majority were Russian, but there were also representatives from many other parts of the world—men and women who had come to fight and die for what they believed was a new beginning and a good cause.

One of the graves belonged to John Reed, an American journalist who witnessed the October Revolution firsthand and wrote about it in a famous book called *Ten Days That Shook the World.* He became a founding member of the American Communist Party. Communism, he said, was one of the "most marvelous adventures" mankind had ever set out on.

In the 70 years that separated the beginning of Reed's adventure from the gleeful demolition of the Berlin Wall, communism came to rule a third of the earth, and the struggle to keep it from spreading obsessed most of the other two-thirds of the world. What was it? How did the communist system work—politically, economically, culturally? How did the communist states deal with each other and the rest of the world? What were communism's successes and why, in the end, did it fail? How did a "marvelous adventure" turn into a murderous wall?

2 Ideas and Ideals

The word "communism" came from the French word "*commun,*" which can be translated as "belonging to all." The idea, if not the word itself, has a long history. Centuries before there were communist parties or communist countries, there were people who believed in the simple idea of sharing the ownership and use of society's wealth equally among all its members. This, they thought, would lead to a fairer, kinder society, one in which cooperation and harmony would replace competition and conflict. People would give what they could and take what they needed.

The Greek **philosopher** Plato thought that such a society would bring out the best in people. So did many of the early Christians. When the sixteenth-century English political and religious leader Sir Thomas More described a perfect society, or *Utopia,* in his book of the same name, he imagined people living communally, sharing their property, and working under the direction of people who had the good of the whole community at heart.

A dream that might come true

Until the end of the eighteenth and early nineteenth centuries this vision was only held by a few isolated individuals. But two great revolutions—the Industrial and the French—changed all that. The **Industrial Revolution,** which began in Great Britain, uprooted millions of people, driving them from the countryside into overcrowded towns where they worked long hours in terrible conditions. The **French Revolution** showed that a society could be turned upside-down and that the rich and powerful could be successfully challenged. As the Industrial Revolution strengthened the desire for change, so the French Revolution encouraged people to believe that such change was possible.

In the early nineteenth century the word **"socialism"** first appeared; like "communism" later in the same century, it described a society built around the shared ownership of wealth. Some utopian socialists, like Robert Owen in Great Britain and Etienne Cabet in the United States, set up model communities—complete villages or small towns—in which people lived according to socialist principles, sharing their work and property.

However, these model communities only affected a small number of people. Most of the new socialists lived in the real world, where they argued and campaigned for a fairer society. Socialism or communism—whatever this fairer society based on shared ownership was called—was beginning to seem like a dream that might come true.

This is a view of New Lanark, the model community founded by Robert Owen in the early nineteenth century.

Karl Marx

One man did more than any other to strengthen this feeling. Karl Marx was a German philosopher and economist, born in 1818, who lived most of his life in England. He was very aware of the unfairness that characterized the newly industrialized countries in the mid-nineteenth century—the huge gap between rich and poor, and the horrible conditions under which many people, including children, worked for very little pay. He wanted to make things right, and he thought, like many others had before him, that the best way to do so was through the creation of a socialist or communist society.

FOR DETAILS ON KEY COMMUNISTS, SEE PAGES 59–60.

But there was a big difference between Marx and his socialist predecessors. They had all wanted a socialist society, but Marx took it further. After years of study and the writing of many books, he believed that a socialist society was actually inevitable, whether one wanted it or not.

A statement of intentions

"Let the ruling classes tremble at a Communistic revolution. The proletarians [workers] have nothing to lose but their chains. They have a world to win. WORKING MEN OF ALL COUNTRIES, UNITE!"

(The final lines of The Communist Manifesto, written by Karl Marx and Friedrich Engels in 1847–1848.)

According to Marx, all of human history had been a history of struggles between ruling classes (those who owned the wealth and had most of the power) and the working classes (those who did most of the work but had little power). He thought that throughout history each ruling class, which dominated a society through force, wealth, or a combination of the two, inevitably created their own opposition. In his time the **capitalists**—the owners of industry, banks, and communications—were the ruling class in the most advanced countries. To make their world work they needed a growing army of ordinary workers. Marx believed that these workers would eventually get so numerous and so fed up with making wealth for other people (while keeping little money for themselves) that they would kick out the capitalists, confiscate their wealth, and rule in their place. Society as a whole would then own what had previously been owned by only a few individuals. Since the workers by this time would make up almost the entire population, their rule was bound to be **democratic**.

Marx had many arguments to back up his prediction of this coming revolution, but he was less certain of what would follow.

He feared that the old rulers would still be dangerous for awhile, and during this period—which he called the dictatorship of the proletariat—the newly victorious workers might have to restrict the old rulers' freedoms. This need would soon pass, however, and society would then enter its socialist phase.

Here Marx distinguished between socialism and communism. Under socialism there would be shared ownership but people would still be rewarded according to how much work they did. Only when there was enough of everything to go around—a situation that Marx, like many nineteenth-century thinkers, thought would happen quickly—would society move into its final perfect stage: communism. Under communism people would give what they were able to give and take what they needed. There would be no conflict, no need for states or armies or police forces. There would be equality between races and genders. People would live in natural harmony.

Karl Marx, the founder of modern communism, is pictured here.

Millions of followers

Marx's theories won over many people. During the final decades of the nineteenth century, "Marxist" political parties were formed around the world. Students like Vladimir Ilyich Ulyanov in Russia—who, as Lenin, would become the first leader of a Marxist revolution—devoured Marx's writings with excitement and anticipation. They all shared Marx's exciting mixture of idealistic hope and absolute certainty. They all believed that communism was right and that history was on their side.

The dream

"A land awaits us where life is beginning anew, where conscious will, intelligence, and an inexorable [unstoppable] love of mankind are in action."

(Russian revolutionary Victor Serge, explaining why he is traveling across Europe in early 1919 to fight for the communists in the **civil war** that followed the Russian Revolution.)

Vladimir Ulyanov is shown here at the age of 25, 6 years before he adopted the name Lenin. After many years of exile in Siberia and Western Europe, he led the second Russian revolution of 1917 and was one of the key figures in building the world's first communist state.

3 Taking Power

Throughout the twentieth century, people who believed in Marx's vision of communism came to power in many countries. The ways in which they seized control often differed. In Russia in 1917, workers and soldiers loyal to Lenin's **Bolshevik** Party (later called the Communist Party) simply seized control of the country's major cities and fought a long **civil war** to win control of the countryside. In China, Mao Zedong's communist soldiers fought a twenty-year civil war against both Chinese and foreign opposition to win power in 1949. This pattern was largely repeated in the countries of Vietnam, Laos, and Cambodia between 1945 and 1975.

FOR DETAILS ON KEY COMMUNISTS, SEE PAGES 59–60.

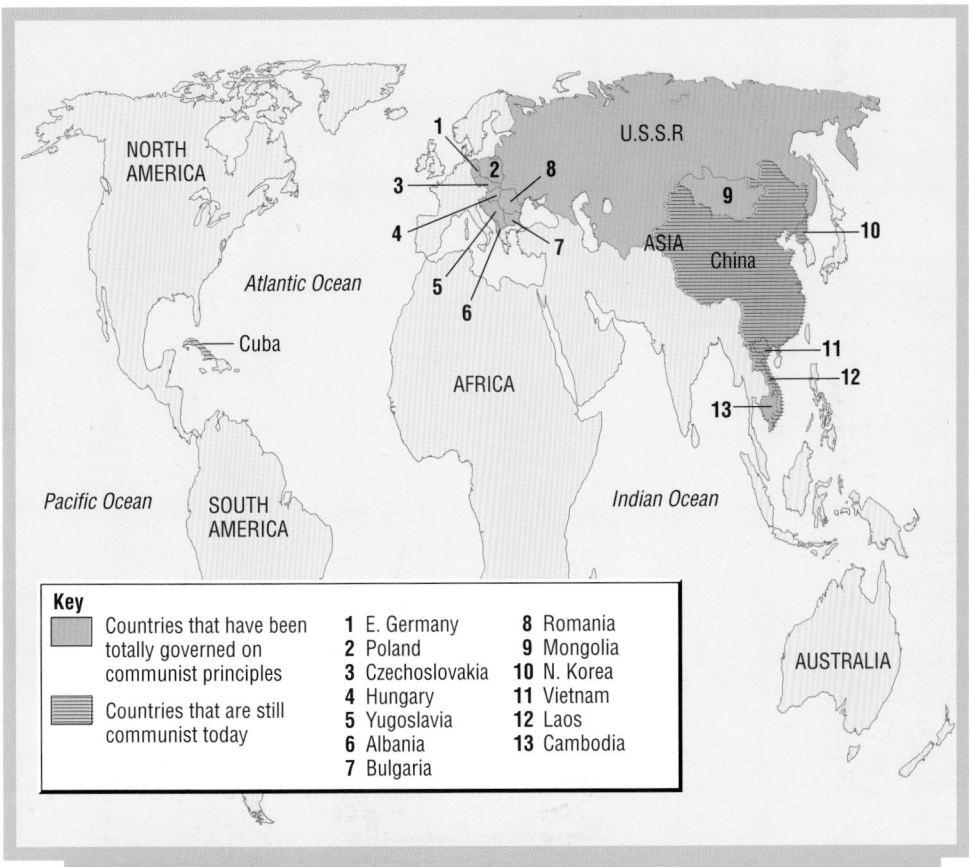

Communist states: past and present.

In Yugoslavia, Albania, and North Korea the communists led the resistance to German, Italian, and Japanese occupying forces during World War II, and seized power when those forces withdrew at the war's end. As the **Cold War** began, the **Soviets** (as the Russians were now called) handed over power to the local communist parties in those east European countries they had occupied during World War II—Poland, Czechoslovakia, Hungary, Bulgaria, Romania, and the eastern zone of Germany. In Cuba, a group of largely non-communist revolutionaries who had seized power in 1959 were converted to communism by a combination of U.S. hostility to their reform policies and help from the Soviets. In 1970, the Chilean communist party was actually voted into power in a general election.

The communist revolution in Russia

There were two revolutions in Russia in 1917. In February, the Tsar and his regime were overthrown and replaced by a temporary government; in October that government was overthrown by the **Bolsheviks**, a Marxist party led by Vladimir Ilyich Lenin. Other prominent members of the Bolsheviks were Leon Trotsky, who organized the armed uprising, and the future leader Joseph Stalin. The Bolsheviks renamed themselves the Communist Party, and for the next 70 years the Russian Empire would be known as the Union of Soviet Socialist Republics (U.S.S.R.), or the Soviet Union.

Most of these takeovers had a great deal of popular support, and for a very simple reason: they offered the promise of turning unfair societies into fairer ones. The Bolsheviks, at the time they seized power, had just received the most votes in the new **democratic** councils (also called "Soviets"), and their policies of withdrawing Russia from World War I and giving land to the **peasants** were supported by a majority of the population. The communists in China, unlike their enemies, the **Guomindang,** were seen as a party of honest men who could unify and modernize the country. In North Korea, Cuba, Yugoslavia, Albania, and Chile, communists were seen as the rescuers of their countries, saving them from foreign occupation or domination.

It was only in eastern Europe that the communists were largely unpopular from the beginning, and that was because they were seen as agents of a foreign power—the Soviet Union.

Soldiers of the 26th of July Movement in Cuba display weapons captured in their war to overthrow the dictator Fulgencio Batista.

How Marx had thought it would happen, and how it did

In the end, it wasn't the way that the communists took power, nor was it the level of popularity enjoyed by the communists that mattered. What really mattered were the circumstances in which they took power, and the fact that these were never the circumstances that Marx had considered appropriate for the building of socialism and communism.

Marx and his followers thought that history unfolded in an orderly manner. Socialism could take over from **capitalism** only when capitalism had developed completely, and had created an advanced industrial economy, turning most of the population into industrial workers. Marx believed that after seizing power, this majority of workers, with their collective, sharing way of working, would take over the enormous wealth created by capitalism and build the socialist society that would one day become a communist paradise. Such revolutions had to happen in the most industrialized countries: Germany, the United States, Great Britain, and France.

By the time Marx died in 1883, it was becoming apparent that things were not going according to plan. Capitalism continued to generate ever-increasing amounts of wealth, and, contrary to Marx's expectations, those in power in the advanced countries made sure that a share of the increase went to the poorest members of the society. The gap between capitalists and workers remained, but it was not getting wider and wider. Everyone was getting richer, the poor included. Over the next 30 years the introduction of pensions for retired people, unemployment pay, and other benefits in countries like Germany, the U.S, and Great Britain improved conditions for the workers even further.

Capitalism was proving much more flexible than Marx had expected, and his followers in these countries found that there were fewer people in favor of a revolution. Capitalism continued to create wealth, and the lives of workers could be improved even more within the existing system, especially now that **trade unions** and democratic politics offered more peaceful ways to press for change. In Germany, which had the largest Marxist **socialist** party in the world, a clear majority of Marx's followers were beginning to argue that they could make the world a fairer place without a revolution. Their decision to take the democratic path to socialism—to try to be elected as a socialist—was eventually followed in all of the most developed countries.

In other countries like Russia, the opposite was happening. Capitalism had barely begun to develop the economies in these countries, so there was no majority working class and no enormous wealth from which to build socialism. Added to this, there was little attempt to improve the conditions of the poor, no democratic government to listen to their complaints, and no possibility of peaceful change. In these societies, the communists' call for revolution grew more popular as the twentieth century unfolded, and became irresistible once the miseries of World War I had been added to the mix.

Round peg and square hole

In 1917, the first Marxist revolution finally took place in Russia, but not in the way that Marx had imagined. Instead of a dominant, majority working class taking over a country wealthy enough to build socialism, a party representing a small working class took over a country mostly made up of **peasants.** Russia had hardly been developed by capitalism, let alone made ready for socialism.

This was absolutely crucial. By seizing power in undeveloped Russia, Lenin and the Bolsheviks were committing themselves to a project that Marx, their inspiration, would have considered impossible. Trying to build **socialism** in Russia was like trying to force a large round peg into a small square hole, and the Bolsheviks, in their attempt to do so, would destroy both the peg and the hole. A bunch of **idealists** would end up creating one of the most oppressive regimes in history. Their dream of a fairer society would turn into a nightmare.

Even at the time, the Bolsheviks were aware of the risk they were running, but they gambled on receiving help from other revolutions in those countries like Germany where Marx had said socialism would be possible. But no other revolutions succeeded, and Russia—or the Soviet Union, as it was now called—remained isolated and alone.

Workers in Russia's far eastern city of Vladivostok march in support of the revolution in 1922.

There was a parting of the ways for the inheritors of the long socialist and communist tradition. Those in the advanced western countries who had decided to follow the peaceful, democratic route to socialism would, from this point on, mostly be known as **socialists** or social democrats. Those who supported Lenin and the Bolsheviks, opting for revolution in a country that was unprepared for the building of socialism, would be known as **Marxist**-Leninists—after Marx and Lenin—or simply communists. They would create the systems of political and economic power that we now know as communism.

4 Keeping Power

Inside the new **Soviet** Union, the Communist Party claimed to represent the industrial working class, but this formed only a small minority of the population. Outnumbered by enemies and potential enemies, the Party had no chance of ruling **democratically**. Instead, it had to make a difficult decision: to either give up power altogether or to establish a **dictatorship.**

End and means

If the communists had followed their own principles they would have given up power. According to **Marxist** theory, Russia needed the sort of **capitalist** development that had happened in western Europe before it could embrace the **socialism** they were promising. Not surprisingly, however, none of the leading communists were in favor of stepping aside.

There were several reasons for this. The first might be described as human nature. Having seized power and then defended it at such a cost through four years of bloody **civil war,** it was asking a lot to expect the Communists to simply walk away. And if they did give up power, to whom would they give it? To the people they had spent their whole lives fighting, people who would bring back all the old unfairness, people who would take the greatest pleasure in having them all shot?

White Russian (anticommunist) troops in Siberia are shown here during the Russian Civil War in 1919.

The second reason for their reluctance to give up power was more worrying. They said that they were democrats at heart, that their eventual aim was a democratic paradise, but during the long years of struggle—marked by years on the run, in hiding,in jail, or in Siberian exile—Lenin and his fellow communists had acquired distinctly dictatorial habits. They had become more like an army than a political party. All the important decisions were made by a small group at the center and handed down as orders. The civil war encouraged and worsened this trend: by 1921 the communists were used to ruling undemocratically.

FOR DETAILS ON KEY COMMUNISTS, SEE PAGES 59–60.

These were not, of course, the reasons the communists themselves gave for their **dictatorial** rule. They justified it as a temporary necessity. If Marx was right, and they believed he was, then history was on their side. They just had to wait for a few years, until revolutions in other countries or their own economic development made socialism and democracy possible in the Soviet Union. If waiting meant that they had to act against their better instincts, then they were prepared to do so. They told themselves that the end (a communist paradise) justified the means (the temporary loss of democracy). They told themselves that they were building an undemocratic bridge into a democratic future.

This idea—of holding political power through a dictatorship while building up a country's wealth for a socialist future—became the very essence of communism. As the decades went by, the temporary fix became permanent. The dreams of a fair, free, and more creative society—which, for a few short years after 1917, seemed to promise so much—slowly but surely gave way to intolerance, harsh rule, and **conformism**. These negative characteristics would come to describe communism, not the ideals that had originally inspired it.

Nikolai Bukharin was a communist Russian leader in the 1920s. He eventually was denounced and executed by Stalin, the state's future dictator.

The Soviet example

In the months after the Russian Revolution, communist parties sprang into existence around the world. As in Russia, many of those who rushed to join these parties were **idealists** who wanted to fight for a fairer world. However, the Soviet domination of the international communist movement meant that most of these idealists soon became infected by the negative characteristics of the example set by the Soviets. Once other communist parties came to power—in China, North Vietnam, North Korea, and eastern Europe—they found themselves facing the same problem the Soviet communists had faced in the 1920s: that of how to build an advanced, socialist society in an undeveloped, **peasant** country. They automatically tried to solve the problem using the same undemocratic solutions.

This natural inclination was reinforced by Soviet pressure. The Soviet way of doing things had become the way things were supposed to be done by **Marxist**-Leninists, the new "party line." The Soviet leadership did not want its people to get the impression that there was another, better road to socialism. Therefore, any Soviet help offered to these new communist governments was on the condition that they followed the Russian example in all the ways that mattered.

How the power crushed the dream

"In pursuit of their dream the **Bolsheviks** had built up an immense and centralized machine of power to which they gradually surrendered more and more of their dream: proletarian [workers'] democracy, the rights of the small nations, and finally their own freedom. They could not dispense with power if they were to strive for the fulfillment of their ideals; but now their power came to oppress and overshadow their ideals."

(Historian Isaac Deutscher, explaining the dilemma in which the Soviet communists found themselves. They needed power to make their political dreams come true, but in order to stay in power they had to sacrifice those dreams.)

5 The One-Party State

The communist belief that history was on their side, that the entire world was inevitably headed for a communist future, was deeply undemocratic. To the communists, it meant that anyone who disagreed with them was misguided or motivated by selfish interests. To allow these people a say in the way the society was run would be harmful to the society as a whole. In some communist states other parties were allowed to exist, but were never allowed to have any real power. These parties were only there to make the system *look* more democratic, not to introduce real **democracy**.

Theory and practice

The same logic was applied to democracy inside communist parties. During the early years of the Russian Revolution, democratic debate and decision-making existed inside the **Soviet** party, but by the mid-1920s factions, or groups, within the party had been banned on the grounds that they were opposition parties in all but name. By the 1930s the idea of a fixed "party line," or policy, that all members had to agree to, had been firmly established. Once this "line" had been decided, it had to be obeyed by everyone, both inside and outside the party.

Who decided it? Almost anyone who wanted to could join the party. In theory, party members all over the country voted members onto local committees. These committees voted members onto the party's **Central Committee.** The Central Committee elected a small executive group or cabinet, usually called the **Politburo** or Praesidium, to make the decisions. Policy suggestions and ideas were supposed to be passed up this chain of command; decisions and instructions were to be passed down.

In practice, all real power was concentrated at the center. Local party members depended on people further up the political chain for their jobs, their promotions, and various privileges, so they were reluctant to rock the boat in any way.

Similarly, those in the **Central Committee** received their jobs and promotions from those in the Politburo, who controlled the centers of economic power as well as the police and armed forces. At the very top of the chain, those in the Politburo relied for their advancement and sometimes even their survival on one man who had concentrated all power in his own hands: Lenin's successor Joseph Stalin in Russia, Mao Zedong in China, and Kim Il Sung in North Korea were in this position for long periods, and were, for all intents and purposes, pure **dictators.** They and they alone made all important decisions that affected their countries.

FOR DETAILS ON KEY COMMUNISTS, SEE PAGES 59–60.

The opening Congress of the Communist International, or **Comintern,** was held in March of 1919.

The role of the secret police and army

The Russian Revolution was only a few months old when Lenin created the **Cheka** (later known by various other names, like the NKVD, GPU, and KGB). This political police force was supposed to defend a revolution fighting for its life against a wide range of violent political enemies, and many hoped that once that fight was won it would be disbanded. However, the communists, though victorious in the Russian **civil war,** remained a small minority, and once they had made the decision to establish their (supposedly temporary) dictatorship, they could not risk eliminating the political police.

A strong political police force would become a key feature in all of the communist states. The secret police was responsible for spying abroad and keeping security at home. At best, these forces helped the leadership stay in touch with what people were thinking. At worst, under Stalin, they became instruments of terror, holding whole countries in the grip of fear.

Felix Dzerzhinsky was the head of the Cheka, the political police force set up by the Russian communists in late 1917 to defend their revolution.

They also kept an eye on the armed forces. Leaders of military units were teamed up with political commissars, party officials who made sure that the "party line" was being obeyed. In China and Vietnam, where communist armies had led the revolution, this was less necessary. During the **Cultural Revolution** in China, Mao Zedong relied on the People's Army to help him overcome opposition to his policies from other party leaders.

The denial of human rights and corruption

The way the system worked in practice,with all the power concentrated in only a few hands, was bound to invite abuses. In theory, communist leaders had to answer to party Central Committees, but in reality they were usually only accountable to their own consciences. They were above the law, and could, within very wide limits, do whatever they liked. They could make far-reaching decisions—like Stalin's to restructure Soviet agriculture in 1928 or Mao's to launch the Great Leap Forward in 1958—

This poster shows Mao Zedong promising rich harvests and technological progress in the Great Leap Forward, a program that in reality only led to famine and great suffering for the Chinese people.

decisions that could result in millions of unnecessary deaths, without fear of retribution or even criticism during their lifetime. Ordinary people had no **human rights.** They had only those rights that the party leaders allowed them.

At the lower levels, there were less serious abuses of power. Party members had access to special shops, special housing and trips abroad. The party became, in almost every way, a new ruling class. Its members did not own industries or huge amounts of property, but they were permitted to use them, which amounted to the same thing. The party official in charge of a car factory could get cars for his party friends, all of whom were doing similar favors connected with their own work.

As the years went by, any lingering **idealism** that was left gradually gave way to widespread **cynicism** and **corruption.** Communist parties that were originally formed to serve the people turned into private clubs designed to serve only their members. Without democracy, without the chance to argue against what was going on, there was no hope of changing it.

Rosa Luxemburg

The Polish communist Rosa Luxemburg was one of the leaders of the German Spartacus League, which became the German Communist Party in 1918. She was a great believer in democracy, and warned the leaders of the Russian Revolution what would happen if they abandoned democracy. The life would be sucked out of all public institutions, she said, leaving government in the hands of a few dozen party leaders and a large, unfeeling bureaucracy. There would be a "brutalization of public life."

Luxemburg herself was murdered during the German communist uprising of January 1919.

6 The Planned Economy

The central feature of **socialism** and communism was the shared ownership of what Marx called the means of production: those things that allowed goods to be made and distributed, such as the factories, tools, and transportation systems. Immediately after seizing power in October of 1917, the **Soviet** communists took these away from the private individuals who had owned them and made them the property of the state. Their intention was to run them for the good of the whole population rather than for the profit of their owners.

FOR DETAILS ON KEY COMMUNISTS, SEE PAGES 59–60.

During the **civil war** that followed the communist takeover, the economy collapsed, money virtually disappeared, and people relied on barter (simple trading) to get what they needed to live. Some communists believed that this was true communism in action, but Lenin knew that such a situation could not last. The people of the new Soviet Union were only sharing their poverty. True communism was about sharing wealth. The key responsibility of the party was to develop the Soviet Union and make it richer.

The key decision

Lenin's **New Economic Policy (NEP),** introduced in 1921, was designed with this in mind. The **peasants,** who formed the vast bulk of the population and who had been given the land they worked on by the new communist government, were encouraged to produce more food, make more money, and spend it on **industrial goods.** This, it was hoped, would stimulate industrial expansion and cause the whole economy to grow.

The plan worked too slowly, however, and other drawbacks soon became apparent. Relying on the peasants gave them power, and the party was unwilling to share power with anyone, let alone those they felt were the most backward part of the population. Also, the NEP seemed like a return to **capitalism** instead of progress toward socialism. Many in the party liked the idea of taking control of the whole economy, and of adopting a harder line toward the countryside.

They argued that if the peasants were paid less than the **market rate** for their crops, then the difference could be invested in industrial expansion and the growth of the whole economy speeded up. In the late 1920s these men, led by Stalin, won the argument and launched what was basically a second revolution, introducing the **collectivization of agriculture** and the central planning of industry.

Soviet leader Joseph Stalin used his power to force his policies on the people of Russia, no matter what the cost.

Collectivization

Not surprisingly, many peasants preferred to eat their surplus crops rather than sell them at a lower price. The Soviet party, faced with accepting a slow rate of growth, decided to take complete control of the countryside. The peasants resisted, and several million died as a result. Many were shot by the political police, and many more suffered cruel treatment in the labor camps of the frozen north. The vast majority, however, died in the famines that followed the peasants' wholesale destruction of their own animals and crops.

Despite the resistance, all of the Soviet Union's privately owned farms had been combined into huge collective farms by 1932. The farmers became paid workers, and their harvest now belonged to the state. There was some good in this. Collective farms, for example, could afford modern equipment that individual farmers could not; but it was vastly outweighed by the bad. Most people in the countryside never forgave the party for the horrors of collectivization, and few tried to make it work.

Collectivization – the human tragedy

"'I am an old Bolshevik,' the GPU [Gosudarstvehnoye Politicheskoye Upravlenie: the political police] Colonel said, almost sobbing. 'I worked in the underground against the Tsar and then I fought in the civil war. Did I do all that in order that I should now surround villages with machine-guns and order my men to fire indiscriminately into crowds of peasants? Oh, no, no!'"

(A Soviet official contrasting his and the revolution's hopes with the terrible reality of collectivization.)

Male and female workers thresh grain on a collectivized farm near the town of Mariupol in the Ukraine, a country which became part of the Soviet Union in 1922.

In China, the leadership tried to soften the blow to the peasants by introducing collectivization a little at a time, hoping to persuade the peasants that it was a good idea. It was only in 1958 that the Communes—even larger versions of the Soviet collective farms—were finally set up. Enthusiasm was high at first, and there were some successes, but in the end the Communes proved to be just as much of a failure as the Soviet collective farms. In the early 1980s, the Communes were divided up into small plots for peasants to rent.

Centrally planned industry

In the Soviet Union's state-owned industry and agriculture, each individual unit—factory or farm—was told what it was expected to produce over a given period of time. The central planners in Moscow decided where the units should get their raw materials, how much the workers should be paid, and to whom they should sell their products and at what price. Every unit's plan was included in a national plan that covered a five-year period.

This system worked well in the beginning. Planning the expansion of basic industries like steel was not a particularly difficult task: the number of different products was small and the work was mostly unskilled, and so the planning was relatively simple. The Soviet economy in the 1930s, as measured by the production of such basic items, grew at a remarkable speed. So did those **developing world** economies which adopted the Soviet system after World War II. Measured by basic industrial development, communism was an economic success, and it was arguably no more inhumane than capitalism during the horrors of the original **Industrial Revolution.**

How industry was planned

If, for example, the central planners decided that a new tractor works should be built in Siberia, they needed to arrange for a supply of steel for the construction of the tractor bodies. For the extra steel to be manufactured, they needed to arrange the mining of extra coal and iron. Both of these materials would need to be transported. This would involve the building of extra trains, which would create the need for even more steel. Extra workers with the right skills would need to be assigned to each operation, and they would need housing, schools for their children, and other facilities. The planners had to make all of these calculations for every part of the economy, and make sure that they were all in balance with each other.

The steelworks at Anshan were a part of China's drive for industrialization in the 1950s.

Of course, such levels of planning led to further restrictions of freedom. People could not change their homes or jobs when they wanted to because the plan relied on them to stay and work where they were. However, there was some compensation for this loss of freedom: the guarantee of a job for everyone. During the Great Depression of the 1930s, when millions of people in the capitalist countries were unemployed, this seemed like one of communism's real advantages.

7 The Totalitarian Society

Communist states went to great lengths to convince their citizens that the "party line," the official view or explanation on any given subject, was the right one. This was partly because they believed it was true, but it was also because they were unwilling to tolerate any opposition to the party's way of doing things or its vision of the future. This sort of society, one that demands complete obedience to the state and allows only one way of seeing things, is usually called **totalitarian.**

Education, media, and arts

Education was given a high priority in communist states, and in non-political subjects like science the standard was usually very high. In subjects with an obvious social or political relevance, the bias was much more evident. History, economics, and politics were only taught from a **Marxist** point of view, and in times of crisis—as, for example, in China during the **Cultural Revolution**—these were almost the only subjects taught.

Attacking the past

"Red Guards all over China took to the streets, giving full vent to their vandalism, ignorance, and fanaticism. They raided people's houses, smashed their antiques, tore up paintings and works of calligraphy [artistic handwriting]. Bonfires were lit to consume books. Museums were raided. Palaces, temples, ancient tombs, statues, pagodas [temples], city walls—anything old was pillaged."

(Jung Chang in her autobiographical novel Wild Swans, describing what happened after Mao Zedong launched a nationwide campaign to "smash up the four olds:" old ideas, old culture, old customs, and old habits.)

There were no privately owned media companies in communist countries, and major newspapers like *Pravda* in Russia and the *People's Daily* in China simply reflected the current "party line" on those issues that the party considered important. Radio, and later, television, did the same. Few different points of view were expressed in news programs or drama, and there was a tendency to fill broadcasting hours with essentially non-political subjects like chess, science, and sports.

There was an explosion of artistic creativity during the early years of the Russian Revolution. The poets Mayakovsky and Esenin, the film-maker Eisenstein, and the architect Tatlin were only the best-known among many figures of international importance. However, the closing down of free debate soon infected the arts, and by the end of the 1920s artists were being ordered to use their work to promote the "party line." This style, which dominated communist arts for the next 50 years, was called "socialist realism," but it was usually far from realistic. In the Soviet Union, writers were forced to produce heroic novels about the struggle to build steel mills in the Siberian wilderness; in China, traveling theater groups told the story of how heroic **peasants,** inspired by thoughts of Mao Zedong, had broken the record for grain harvested in a single day.

FOR DETAILS ON KEY COMMUNISTS, SEE PAGES 59–60.

In later years, as their populations grew less willing to accept such a one-sided view of reality, the communist states allowed artists more freedom. In some European countries like the Soviet Union and Czechoslovakia, there was a significant revival of creativity, particularly in cinema.

This is a still from Sergei Eisenstein's film Alexander Nevsky (1938). Eisenstein was the best known of the early Soviet filmmakers.

Religion and the personality cult

Religion was downplayed by Communism. Marx called religion "the opium of the people," meaning that it was a drug to keep them from thinking. Most communists felt that religion's promise of a heavenly afterlife was just a trick to keep the poor happy on earth. Although religious worship was rarely banned in communist countries, it was made extremely difficult in most of them.

At the same time, the communists turned their own leaders into virtual gods. Lenin was the first to be given this treatment when his body was embalmed (preserved) and placed in a tomb in Red Square for people to view for years to come. His writings became like holy books and his picture appeared everywhere. Right up to the end of the Soviet Union, Lenin had a god-like status that many feel he himself would have found laughable.

A similar **personality cult** was created for Stalin while he was still alive. His face covered entire buildings and was even projected onto the clouds. Writers celebrated his "universal genius." Hospitals, rivers, towns, and factories were named after him.

Stalin's head is projected onto clouds above Moscow's Red Square.

After Stalin, the Soviet communists stopped building up their leaders in such a way, but the practice continued in other communist countries. During China's **Cultural Revolution,** Mao allowed himself to be turned into a virtual god. Millions of people chanted from the famous *Little Red Book* of his sayings. Children were encouraged to believe that "Father is dear, mother is dear, but Chairman Mao is the dearest of all." In North Korea the worship of leader Kim Il Sung was taken to even greater extremes.

Over the top?

North Korean leader Kim Il Sung was known as Great Leader throughout his more than 40 years in power. From the 1960s onwards, every North Korean adult wore a badge bearing his face, and by the late 1980s there were 34,000 monuments to him scattered around North Korea. That number did not include all of the benches on which he had once sat, and which were now protected with glass. Kim was followed everywhere by an assistant who wrote down his every word, and citizens were occasionally sent to prison for accidentally sitting on a newspaper bearing his photograph.

Holding back the past

The party outlawed religion partly out of their own beliefs, and partly because it wished to deny people the opportunity of hearing a different point of view. The non-communist past also offered a source of comparison, and some communist states tried to discourage their citizens from looking back in time. Generally speaking, Soviet communists had little to fear from comparisons with the Russian past, which was rarely kinder than their own rule. Russia's churches, for example, were not all torn down. In China, however, there was a conscious effort to destroy the past during the Cultural Revolution, and much of the country's heritage was lost.

However, this cultural vandalism paled in comparison to what happened in Cambodia, which was renamed Democratic Kampuchea during the rule of the communist Khmer Rouge (1975–1978). The Khmer Rouge made the decision to erase the nation's memory by executing all those, like teachers and writers, who carried the knowledge of previous centuries in their minds. The Khmer Rouge said their aim was to restart history with a blank slate at "year zero." Almost a third of Cambodia's six million people were killed.

This mound of skulls, found in an abandoned Cambodian schoolhouse, is made up of the many victims of the Khmer Rouge.

Opposition

Despite the attempt to impose only one way of looking at things, there was always at least some opposition to communist rule. Many individuals were arrested and jailed, but mass protests were rare, and violent protests even rarer. When violence was used—as, for example, during a revolt by sailors at Kronstadt in the Soviet Union (1921) or the national uprising against Soviet intervention in Hungary (1956)—the rebels were quickly overpowered. Even when the opposition was peaceful—as it was in Czechoslovakia during the "Prague Spring" of 1968 and in China during the student protests that ended so tragically in Tiananmen Square (1989)—the country's armed forces were called out to crush the protesters.

Most opposition was kept within relatively safe bounds. Writers would circulate political articles and stories to friends, and sometimes try to smuggle them out to the **capitalist** world for publication. Most ordinary people expressed their disenchantment by cheating the state whenever they could and by retreating into family life and leisure. It may have been okay to express only one point of view in public, but the party rarely interfered with what people thought or said in their own homes.

Tanks of the People's Liberation Army rumble toward a defenseless student in China's Tiananmen Square in June of 1989.

8 Foreign Relations

When it came to dealing with the rest of the world, the new communist governments in the Soviet Union had two contradictory aims in mind. On the one hand, it saw the governments of **capitalist** countries as its natural enemies, and was eager to help the people of those countries overthrow those governments and replace them with communist ones. They considered it their international duty to promote other revolutions, and as early as 1919 they set up the Communist International **(Comintern)** to organize a global support network.

Lenin addresses the Second Congress of the Communist International in 1920.

On the other hand, they could not afford to provoke and antagonize other countries to the point where their own revolution was threatened. As the years went by, and priority was given to building up the **Soviet** economy, the need for trade and foreign technology made it necessary to improve relations, at least on the surface. Some support was still given to **revolutionary** movements elsewhere, but in general the Soviet communists became much more interested in proving that their own system was better at producing economic growth than was the capitalist system.

A common enemy

In the 1930s the security of this inward-looking Soviet Union was threatened by the rise of Nazi Germany. Nazism, like Soviet communism, was a **totalitarian** system that did not tolerate other beliefs, but in other ways the two ideologies were almost opposites. Communists believed in government ownership, science, internationalism, racial and gender equality; Nazis, on the other hand, believed in private ownership, **romanticism, nationalism, racism,** and keeping women in the home. Added to this list of basic differences was the fact that the Nazi leader Adolf Hitler made it clear that he had plans to conquer large areas of the Soviet Union for future German settlement.

Stalin, the Soviet communist leader, did all he could to deflect this threat. He tried to form an alliance with the western powers of Britain and France, but was rejected. He then signed the Nazi-Soviet Pact with the Germans, in which the two states promised not to attack each other. Stalin hoped that this would provide him with enough time to re-arm the Soviet Union while the Germans were occupied in the West. He bought himself only two years, but they may have been crucial.

FOR DETAILS ON KEY COMMUNISTS, SEE PAGES 59–60.

Germany finally attacked the Soviet Union in June of 1941, and during the rest of World War II Stalin found himself in an uneasy alliance with the capitalist West. Once the war was over and Nazism had been defeated, the alliance crumbled because the two sides had few shared interests. Still, in places like eastern Europe, either capitalism or communism had to triumph: there was no middle ground. Between 1945 and 1948 the Soviets, worried about future attacks on themselves from the area, made sure that it was communism. The United States thought this was the first step in a program of communist expansion and took steps of their own. For the next 40 years, relations between the United States and the Soviet Union—between the **democratic** West and communism—would be marked by suspicion and hostility.

A Red Army soldier hoists the Soviet flag above the ruins of the German parliament building after the capture of Berlin in May of 1945.

The Russo-German Front during World War II (1941–45)

In the months that followed the German attack on the Soviet Union in June of 1941, the **Bolshevik** army was forced to surrender huge areas of western Russia and the Ukraine. Fortunately, one of the key elements of the first two five-year development plans in the 1930s had been the relocation of many Soviet factories to the east of the country, and the weapons produced in these factories were important in holding and then driving back the Germans. Through 1944 and 1945 the Bolsheviks faced 90 percent of the German army, while the Western powers in France and Italy faced only 10 percent. Estimates suggest that around 20 million Soviet citizens died in World War II, more than all of the other Allied countries put together.

The Cold War

The **Cold War** never became an actual war for one reason—the invention of nuclear weapons in the 1940s. Once the Soviets had exploded their own atom bomb in 1949, neither the United States nor the Soviet Union could risk what came to be known as Mutually Assured Destruction (MAD). Each continued to improve the number and quality of its bombs and bomb delivery systems, but neither ever expected to get so far ahead in this arms race that it could actually risk starting a nuclear war.

Because they did not dare to engage in military conflict, the Soviet Union and the United States competed politically and economically. In the 1950s and early 1960s, people on both sides became convinced, mostly because the Soviets had made many achievements in space, that the Soviet economy was catching up with the U.S. economy. It was not until the 1980s that it became obvious that this was never going to happen. In the meantime, the two governments and their allies competed in the **developing world** for friends and influence. On the communist side, the Russians helped build such projects as the Aswan High Dam in Egypt, the Chinese built the Tanzam railway in central Africa, and the Cubans offered both military and civilian help—like doctors and teachers—to many other developing world countries.

During the half-century following World War II, there were many examples of conflicts involving communist parties or armies around the world, but the Russian communists stuck to the decision they had made in the 1920s, putting the interests of their own country ahead of helping out fellow communists. They supported the Cubans economically and they supplied arms to friends like the North Koreans and North Vietnamese, but the only time they became militarily involved in a full-scale war to help foreign communists was in Afghanistan during the 1980s. In that case they intervened because they were concerned that the war might spill across the border into their own territories, not because they were feeling particularly generous.

Two Vietnamese communists open fire on U.S. aircraft attacking their village in South Vietnam in April of 1969.

This reluctance to support other revolutions was one of the main reasons for the breakdown of the relationship between the Soviet Union and China in the 1960s. At this point, both the Chinese and the Cubans were eager to spread **revolution** to the rest of the developing world and they were angry with the Soviets for refusing to help them. From the early 1970s, however, they followed the Soviet example, preferring their own security and economic well-being to running the risks of supporting world revolution.

9 Inflexibility and Collapse

The tremendous growth in the Soviet Union's basic industries in the 1930s, and the country's dominant role in defeating Nazi Germany in World War II, seemed, for a little while, to back up the communists' claim that they were creating a valid alternative to **capitalism.** But as the post-war world unfolded, the gap between communist ideals and reality began to grow more and more obvious. There might have been economic growth and scientific advances to boast about, but there was little else. Communist societies in the Soviet Union and Eastern Europe were much less free, much less creative, and not noticeably fairer than the capitalist societies of western Europe and North America. If communism was to pose a real threat to capitalism, it needed to clean up its act and reform itself.

Khrushchev and the first attempts at reform

The first leader to attempt this was the Soviet leader Nikita Khrushchev, who rose to power after Stalin's death in 1953. He believed that the communist system created by Lenin and Stalin was basically sound, but blamed Stalin for creating a climate of terror that had stifled initiative throughout Soviet society. Khrushchev released some prisoners, stressed collective (joint) leadership, and introduced a few limited economic reforms. The party's grip was slightly relaxed.

FOR DETAILS ON KEY COMMUNISTS, SEE PAGES 59–60.

This had two important consequences. First, the economy remained sluggish because the party's grip was still too tight. Second, even this slightest relaxation produced a challenge to the party's rule. There was no trouble in the Soviet Union, but in both Hungary and Poland in 1956 the introduction of Khrushchev's very minor measures proved enough to put the whole system in danger. In Poland, matters were solved peacefully by a simple change of communist leaders, but in Hungary, the Soviet Union had to use tanks to reinstate a government it approved of.

Watched by his fellow Hungarians, a man burns a portrait of Soviet leader Joseph Stalin during the 1956 uprising.

Over the next 35 years, this pattern of events would become a key feature of European communism. The obvious need for reforms would push the party into introducing them, but the reforms would end up threatening the party itself. Communism was basically unable to be reformed.

China

In the 1950s, China went through many of the same experiences that the Soviet Union had been through in the 1930s. Heavy industry was expanded through five-year plans and agriculture was **collectivized.** By the end of the decade Mao Zedong was growing impatient, and in 1958 he introduced an accelerated program of growth called the Great Leap Forward. This program, which tried to substitute massive effort and enthusiasm for proper planning, created chaos. This chaos was especially felt in the countryside, where a resulting famine killed around twenty million people between 1959 and 1962.

As this disaster unfolded in 1960, Mao was forced to hand over control of the economy to moderate politicians Liu Shaoqi and Deng Xiaoping. However, his god-like status as the creator of the revolution meant that he remained very popular in both the party and the country. Liu and Deng got the economy moving again, but Mao believed that they were stressing economic progress at the expense of communist ideals, and taking the party away from ordinary people. In 1966, with the support of the People's Army and the units of enthusiastic young Red Guards, he launched the **Cultural Revolution** to give the revolution back to the people and to put himself back in control. Another period of chaos followed, this one lasting almost a decade, in which many millions of people were killed and many more millions had their lives turned inside out.

Officials in dunce caps are paraded through Beijing by Red Guards during the Chinese Cultural Revolution.

After Mao's death in 1976, Deng Xiaoping was brought back to lead the country. He, like Khrushchev, tried to relax the economic system without putting the party's rule at risk. In the 1980s he relaxed control too much, and then had to suppress two student protests by force. When he sent tanks against students in Beijing's Tiananmen Square, it was witnessed on television sets around the world. Deng Xiaoping's successors have continued with the same delicate balancing act between allowing the economy to grow and maintaining the party's control.

Cuba and Czechoslovakia

Mao was not the only communist who believed that Khrushchev and the later Soviet leaders had lost touch with the **idealism** that had made communism so appealing in the first place. In the 1960s, the first decade of the revolution in Cuba, a deliberate effort was made there to appeal to people's better, more idealistic nature instead of their greed for possessions. The Cubans also stressed the old communist idea of helping other revolutionaries around the world. Che Guevara, the Argentinian who had been one of Cuban leader Fidel Castro's most important partners in creating and running the revolution, left Cuba to fight for more revolutions in both Africa and South America. He was killed in Bolivia in 1967.

A modern adventurer

"I believe in armed struggle as the only solution for people who are fighting for freedom, and act according to this belief. Many will call me an adventurer, and I am, but of a different kind—one who risks his skin in order to prove his convictions. Perhaps this will be my last letter. This is not my intention, but it is within the realm of logical possibility. If so, I send you a last embrace."

(From Che Guevara's letter to his family, on his departure from Cuba in 1965. Guevara's life and death offered proof that not all communists had lost sight of communism's original ideals.)

There was also a strong strand of idealism in the events that overtook Czechoslovakia in 1967–1968. These, like the events in Hungary twelve years earlier, grew out of reforms that had been introduced in the Soviet Union and had quickly spiralled out of control. The Czechoslovaks, under party leader Alexander Dubcek, believed that more **democracy** would be better and would make the economic reforms more effective. They thought the party could control this process, but the Soviets were not prepared to risk their being wrong. In August of 1968, the Soviets sent in tanks to stop the Czechoslovakian experiment.

Alexander Dubcek was First Secretary of the Czechoslovak Communist Party and the leader of the 1968 "Prague Spring."

The system self-destructs

By the 1970s, communism around the world was stuck in a deepening rut. The promise of economic growth, which had once offered some compensation for the absence of freedom, was rapidly evaporating. The planned economy had worked well as an engine of basic development, but it was becoming obvious that it was unable to deliver the goods in a sophisticated consumer economy. Delivering ten million shoes was one thing; delivering ten million shoes of various sizes, colors, and styles to 200 million consumers was something entirely different. There were just too many calculations for the planners to make.

Meanwhile, increased athletic and cultural contacts gave the Soviet people a better idea of what life was really like in the West. This increased the pressure for greater freedom in politics, the arts, and life in general. Radical reform was becoming inevitable, but until 1985, the party still shrank from the consequences of introducing it. Then Mikhail Gorbachev took over as the Soviet leader and finally introduced the major changes that had been needed for so long.

Russia's first post-communist leader, Boris Yeltsin (left), shares a word with the last leader of the Soviet Union, Mikhail Gorbachev.

As the party had always feared, real reform led to collapse. Gorbachev could not carry through his policy of *perestroika* (restructuring of the system) without fatally weakening the power of the Communist Party. Between 1988 and 1991, the party lost the ability to impose its will on eastern Europe, the non-Russian areas of the Soviet Union, and finally Russia itself. A far from perfect democracy took over from one-party rule, and free enterprise replaced the planners. By 1991, there was not a communist state left in Europe.

Power to the people

"The essence of perestroika is for people to feel they are the country's master."

(Mikhail Gorbachev in 1986, explaining that the party must become more democratic.)

10 Communism in the 21st Century

Ten years after the collapse of the Soviet Union, communist parties still held power in several countries, but many doubted whether any of these countries could still be considered truly communist.

The prime example was China, the world's most populated country. Under Deng Xiaoping's successors, the Chinese party held on to its monopoly of political power. At the same time, it promoted the role of **market forces** in the economy by expanding private ownership and encouraging China's citizens to enrich themselves. Large increases in wealth temporarily dampened the enthusiasm for political reform, but in the long run greater economic freedom seemed certain to have political consequences.

The gospel according to Deng

"It does not matter whether a cat is black or white as long as it catches mice."

(Chinese leader Deng Xiaoping in the 1980s, explaining that the party was willing to consider any methods of achieving economic growth, no matter how uncommunist they might be.)

Chinese President Jiang Zemin is pictured here during a visit to Moscow in July of 2001. Jiang and his colleagues in the Chinese leadership have continued with the business-friendly policies introduced by Deng Xiaoping.

The situations in Vietnam and Cuba were similar. In both countries, the ruling parties tried to invigorate their economies by enlarging the role of market forces without giving up political control, and by introducing a measure of **capitalism** without introducing **democracy.** In Cuba, the government had more support than in other communist countries for a number of reasons. The revolution's undoubted successes, particularly in health care and education, were credited to the government, while many of its failures were blamed on the U.S. policy of refusing to trade with Cuba for 40 years. Whether the regime's popularity would survive the death of its founder Fidel Castro remained an open question.

FOR DETAILS ON KEY COMMUNISTS, SEE PAGES 59–60.

Developing-world prospects

The **developing world** at the beginning of the 21st century was full of countries with similarities to the Russia of 1917: mass poverty, unfairness, and economies dominated by foreigners and a small number of local elites. Given this, the possibility that political parties which promised increased development, greater fairness, and strict controls on foreign business might gather support and seize power was fairly likely. Some of them would no doubt call themselves communist.

If such 21st century communists did seize power, they would encounter enormous problems. They would face the same dilemmas as the **Bolsheviks** had a century before them—to abandon power or to abandon democratic principles, and to develop at a snail's pace or on the backs of an unwilling **peasantry.** Whichever decisions they made, the economic difficulties and human cost would be huge.

Cuba's President Fidel Castro, who came to power after leading a revolution to victory in 1959, is one of the world's longest-serving leaders. This photo was taken in September of 2001.

Such 21st century communists would probably also face the hostility and power of the capitalist world. The communist government elected by the people of Chile in 1970 was eventually brought down by a number of reasons, including U.S. support for anti-communist groups in the Chilean Army. The same pressures were applied to the partly communist government of Nicaragua in the 1980s. It is possible that these pressures would be applied again should the need arise.

Anti-communism in action

"Not a nut or a bolt will be allowed to reach Chile under Allende . . . We shall do all in our power to condemn Chile and the Chileans to utmost deprivation and poverty, a policy designed for a long time to come to accelerate the hard features of a Communist society in Chile."

(Edward Korry, U.S. Ambassador to Chile, predicting what his country would do in the event of a victory for the communist coalition led by Salvador Allende in the Chilean election of 1970.)

In the developed world

In ex-communist European countries, the old communist parties lingered on with varying degrees of success. In those that were adapting better to capitalism—like the Czech Republic—communism was no more than a bad memory, but in those like Russia, where the transition was proving to be a painful process, people sometimes tended to forget communism's bad points and remember the good. Raging unemployment and rising levels of crime made them long for the old job security, and law and order of Stalin's day.

In the developed countries of western Europe and North America, the communism of Lenin and Stalin never came to power, either peacefully or through revolution. These were the countries that Marx believed would follow the path he mapped out—through revolution, the **dictatorship** of the working class, and **socialism**—to the promised paradise of communism. But the capitalism of the **free market** continued to thrive. After the collapse of European communism at the end of the 1980s, capitalism's victory seemed complete.

The problems confronting capitalism in the 21st century—the further widening of the gulf between rich and poor, escalating **terrorism,** and the threat of environmental catastrophe—may create the need for a more **idealistic** and sharing kind of society than the one that existed at the turn of the millennium. Such a society might even be communist in the old meaning of the word, before Marxism. It is quite certain, however, that it will not look anything like the communism that played such a large role in the history of the twentieth century.

11 So, What Is Communism?

Communism was—and in some parts of the world, still is—that system of political, economic, and social organization that spread across a third of the world from its birthplace in Russia. Communist takeovers were often fueled by **idealism,** but this was soon swept aside by the practical need to produce economic growth in previously undeveloped economies. The system that evolved to meet this challenge in Russia during the 1920s and 1930s became the model for all of the other communist countries to follow, at least in their early years. It is this system that we now associate with the much older word "communism."

The system had several features. Only one political party—the Communist Party—was allowed to hold real power. Decisions within this party were generally made at the highest levels and passed down as instructions or orders. Ordinary people had a few limited ways of making their feelings and thoughts known to the leadership, but it was not a **democratic** system in any sense of the word. The political police played a crucial role in keeping the party informed about what the people were thinking, and in clamping down on any anti-government activity.

Crushed hopes

"We **revolutionaries,** who aimed to create a new society,'the broadest democracy of the workers,' had unwittingly, with our hands, constructed the most terrifying State machine conceivable; and when, with revulsion, we realized the truth, this machine, driven by our friends and comrades, turned on us and crushed us."

(Russian revolutionary Victor Serge, writing in the 1940s.)

Another key feature—many would say the central defining feature of communism—was the creation of an almost completely government-owned economy in which almost all activities were planned in advance. This economic **dictatorship** was connected with the political dictatorship to the point where neither could be reformed without the other.

Other aspects of social life—like education, sports, the arts, and the media—were controlled by the party, and used to advertise and promote the party's version of reality. Communist achievements and **capitalist** failures were taught and reported, while communist failures and capitalist achievements were rarely mentioned. In some communist countries, a **personality cult** was built up around individual leaders which took this disregard for truth even further. There was, in these cases, an obvious attempt to create an almost religious atmosphere. The communists were doing exactly what they had criticized organized religions for doing: offering a god and a wonderful future in return for a difficult life in the present.

This photo shows the traditional May Day celebrations in Moscow's Red Square in 1954.

Why it lasted so long

FOR DETAILS ON KEY COMMUNISTS, SEE PAGES 59–60.

Despite the lack of **democracy** and the terrible hardships, there were many believers in communism. In many cases, communist states were better than what had gone before. Lenin's Soviet Union, Mao's China, and Castro's Cuba were no less democratic than the regimes that they had replaced, and seemed to offer much more to the masses of ordinary people. Not all of these positive comparisons were with the past. For example, Cubans compared themselves with other Latin Americans, and even though many resented Castro's dictatorial ways, they also took pride in having better health care services and higher literacy rates than all of their capitalist neighbors.

In the Soviet Union, communism was bolstered by national pride in the country's superpower status. In countries like China, Vietnam, and Cuba, one feature of the communist takeover was to get rid of foreign influence; success in this regard sparked a rise in national pride that was slow to fade. The opposite was the case in Eastern Europe. Communism's association with Soviet domination made it even more unpopular than it would have been otherwise.

An experiment that failed?

It is hard to exaggerate the impact of communism in the twentieth century. It inspired many with its vision and condemned many more to hardship and suffering. Some, however, might argue the same things of capitalism over the last two centuries. What really distinguished communism was the enormous gulf that developed between the theory and the practice, the promise and the reality. There were impressive communist achievements in the fields of basic economic development and science, but in most communist countries these were eventually outweighed by later economic stagnation and the loss of democracy.

The disciples of Marx and Lenin who set out to make the world a better and fairer place for everyone ended up creating one of the

Shortages of bread and other goods were common in the Soviet Union, but they continued even after the end of communism in Russia, as this photo taken in 1991 shows.

least efficient, least democratic, and least humane systems in modern history. Communism's failure in Europe and the reasons for it should be understood and remembered, but so should the fact that millions of people around the world believed it to be a cause worth fighting and dying for.

It remains to be seen what will happen to the communist societies in existence today.

Communism and capitalism

"What is the difference between capitalism and communism? Capitalism is the exploitation of man by man; communism is the reverse."

(A popular saying in Poland during the years of communist rule, which expressed the widely held belief that the two systems were as bad as each other.)

Timeline

1818	Birth of Karl Marx in Trier, Germany
1848	Marx's and Engels' *Communist Manifesto* is published
1867	The first volume of Marx's key work *Capital* (*Das Kapital*) is published
1883	Death of Karl Marx
1893	The Marxist Russian Social **Democratic** Labor Party (RSDLP) is founded
1898	The RSDLP splits into **Bolshevik** and Menshevik factions
	Birth of Mao Zedong
1905	During a year of rebellion the first **soviets** appear in Russian cities
1914–18	World War I
1917	The first communist revolution takes place in Russia
1918–21	Russian civil war
1919	Formation of **Comintern** (or Communist International)
1921	Kronstadt rebellion
	Lenin introduces the **New Economic Policy (NEP)**
	The Chinese Communist Party is founded
1924	Death of Lenin
1927	Trotsky exiled
1928	Stalin introduces the first five-year development plan
1929–33	Soviet **collectivization of agriculture**
1934–35	The Long March of the Chinese Communist Party
1934–38	Stalin's campaign of violence and intimidation within the Soviet Union
1939–45	World War II
1941	Nazi Germany attacks the Soviet Union
1945–48	Eastern European countries are forced to accept communist governments
1947	Cold War begins
1949	People's Republic of China is founded
1950–53	Korean War
1953	Death of Stalin
1954	France expelled from Vietnam by communists

1956	Khrushchev attacks Stalin in a "secret speech"
	Soviet troops crush the Hungarian rebellion
1958	Mao launches the Great Leap Forward
1959	Cuban revolution
1961	Construction of the Berlin Wall begins
1964	Khrushchev is forced out by his colleagues
1966	Mao launches the **Cultural Revolution**
1967	Che Guevara is captured and murdered in Bolivia
1968	"Prague Spring" in Czechoslovakia
	Soviet and other allied armed forces invade Czechoslovakia
1970	Communists win the election in Chile
1973	Military coup overthrows the communist government in Chile
1975	Vietnam is reunited as a communist state
	Khmer Rouge take over in Cambodia
1976	Death of Mao Zedong
1978	Deng Xiaoping introduces far-reaching reforms
1979	Sandinista (communist) victory in Nicaragua
	Vietnamese invade Cambodia to overthrow the Khmer Rouge
	Soviet Union invades Afghanistan in support of its communist government
1985	Gorbachev takes over as Soviet leader
1989	Pro-**democracy** demonstrations in Beijing are crushed by troops
	Eastern Europe abandons communism
	Fall of the Berlin Wall
1991	Soviet Union breaks up; Gorbachev resigns
1997	Death of Deng Xiaoping
1999	Cuba's Fidel Castro celebrates 40 years in power

Sources for Further Research

Books

Downing, David. *Joseph Stalin.* Chicago: Heinemann Library, 2001.

Downing, David. *Vladimir Ilyich Lenin* Chicago: Heinemann Library, 2002.

Higgenbottom, Trevor. *China.* Chicago: Heinemann Library, 2000.

Morrison, Marion. *Cuba.* New York.: Raintree Steck-Vaughn, 1998.

Press, Petra. *Fidel Castro: An Unauthorized Biography.* Chicago: Heinemann Library, 1999.

Rady, Martyn C. *Collapse of Communism in Eastern Europe.* New York: Raintree Steck-Vaughn, 1995.

Ritchie, Nigel. *Communism.* New York: Raintree Steck-Vaughn, 2001.

Schlesinger, Arthur M. *Alexander Dubcek—Czechoslovak Political Leader.* Broomall, Penn.: Chelsea House Publishers, 1991.

Stewart, Whitney. *Deng Xiaoping: Leader in a Changing China.* Minneapolis, Minn.: Lerner Publishing Group, 2001.

Taylor, David. *The Cold War.* Chicago: Heinemann Library, 2001.

Warren, James A. *Cold War: The American Crusade Against the Soviet Union and World Communism, 1945-1990.* New York: Harper Collins Children's Book Group, 1996.

Websites

http://www.coldwar.org/

http://www.cnn.com/SPECIALS/cold.war/

http://www.cnn.com/resources/newsmakers/world/namerica/castro.html

Key Figures in the History of Communism

Castro, Fidel. (1927–). Castro led the 26th of July Movement in Cuba that overthrew the dictator Fulgencio Batista after a short guerrilla war in 1959. Castro announced that he had become a communist in 1961, and has led Cuba ever since.

Deng Xiaoping. (1904–97). Deng was one of the more moderate leaders of the Chinese party in the 1950s and early 1960s. Disgraced during the **Cultural Revolution,** he was brought back to repair the economy in the 1970s, and continued to serve as the real leader of China until his death.

Engels, Friedrich. (1820–95). Engels was Marx's friend and intellectual partner. He co-wrote *The Communist Manifesto* and wrote several important works of his own.

Gorbachev, Mikhail. (1931–). Gorbachev took over the leadership of the Soviet Union in 1985 and introduced far-reaching reforms which ultimately undermined the power of the party, the unity of the country, and his own position. He resigned in 1991.

Guevara, Ernesto "Che." (1928–67). Che was an Argentinian who took part in the Cuban guerrilla uprising led by Fidel Castro. He served in the Cuban government for several years, but then left Cuba to take part in revolutions in central Africa and Bolivia. He was caught and murdered in 1967.

Ho Chi Minh. (1890–1969). Ho founded the IndoChina Communist Party in 1930, and became the communist president of North Vietnam in 1954. From 1959 until his death, he supported the South Vietnamese communists in their struggle against a government supported by the United States.

Kim Il Sung. (1912–94). Kim led the armed resistance to the Japanese occupation of Korea in the 1930s and 1940s. In 1945, he became the leader of Soviet-occupied North Korea, a position that he held until his death.

Lenin, Vladimir Ilyich. (1870–1924). Lenin was the leader of the first **Marxist** revolution (the second Russian Revolution of 1917). Leader of the **Bolshevik** wing of the Russian Social Democratic Labor Party since 1903, he persuaded his party to seize power.

Mao Zedong. (1893–1976). Mao was a founding member of the Chinese Communist Party in 1921, and its leader from the mid-1930s. After the communist victory in 1949 he supervised the construction of a Soviet-style economy and tried to accelerate growth through the Great Leap Forward in 1958. This failed, but in 1966 he launched the Cultural Revolution against party bureaucracy. This proved to be another disaster for Chinese economic development, and in the last years of his life, Mao was once again forced to share power with more moderate colleagues.

Marx, Karl. (1818–83). Marx was the German **philosopher,** economist, and political scientist whose theories of social development helped to inspire both **socialism** and communism. He was active in politics, and a founder of the First International, an association of **trade unions** of different countries.

Pol Pot (c.1925–98). Pol Pot was the leader of Cambodia's Khmer Rouge regime in the late 1970s. His policies of "reconstruction" were responsible for millions of deaths.

Stalin, Joseph. (1878–1953). Stalin became General Secretary of the Soviet party in 1921, and used that position to rid himself of potential opponents. By the end of the 1920s, when he launched the five-year plans and the **collectivization of agriculture,** he was the country's undisputed **dictator.** In the 1930s, he created a climate of terror in which millions of people were imprisoned or killed, but he proved a competent military leader during World War II.

Trotsky, Leon. (1879–1940). Trotsky organized an uprising against the Tsar in Russia in October of 1917 and led the **Red Army** to victory in the civil war. After Lenin died, he unsuccessfully opposed the rise of Stalin. He was exiled in 1927 and eventually murdered by an agent of Stalin in 1940.

Glossary

Bolshevik one of the two political parties that emerged from the 1903 split in the Russian Social Democratic Labor Party. *Bolshevik* is Russian for "those with a majority."

capitalism economic system in which the production and distribution of goods depend on private wealth and profit-making

capitalist someone who owns capital (money or property), and combines it with other people's work to make profits

Central Committee after 1917, the committee elected by local Communist Party committees throughout the Soviet Union. This in turn elected a smaller ruling committee, the Politburo.

Cheka Extraordinary Commission for Combating Counter-Revolution and Sabotage: the political police force created by Lenin in December of 1917

civil war war between different groups in one country

Cold War name given to the hostility that existed between the capitalist and communist worlds between 1947 and the late 1980s

collectivization of agriculture creation of large, jointly-owned farms by combining small farms that had previously been privately owned

Comintern Communist International, an organization formed by the world's communist parties with the aim of promoting world revolution

conformism going along with the existing customs or rules; not wanting to rock the boat

corruption immoral practices like bribery or fraud

Cultural Revolution decade of political chaos and instability in China, unleashed by Mao Zedong in 1966 with the support of the Red Guards and People's Army. Mao's aim was to weaken those in the party who wished to follow a Soviet-style policy of economic progress at the expense of grassroots involvement. The conflict was not resolved until after Mao's death in 1976.

cynicism tendency to expect the worst from people

democracy political system in which governments are regularly elected by the mass of the people, or a country in which this system exists

developing world poorer countries of the world

dictatorship government by an individual (called a dictator) or a small group that does not allow the mass of the people any say in their government

embargo government policy of not trading with a particular country

fascism dictatorial system of government originating in Italy, which was later known for its aggressive nationalism. Nazism was one type of fascism.

free market economy in which individuals rather than governments make the decisions about which goods and services are produced, and how they are bought and sold

French Revolution political upsurge in France that began with the storming of the Bastille prison in 1789, and developed into an assault on the upper classes, ending with the execution of the king and many aristocrats in the 1793–94 reign of terror

Guomindang (Kuomintang) Chinese nationalist movement led by Chiang Kai-shek, which lost to the communists in the Chinese Civil War

human rights rights that should belong to any person

idealism belief that the world can be made a better place

industrial goods goods made from raw materials, or other goods made in factories or workshops

Industrial Revolution change from a primarily agricultural economy to one based on large-scale production in factories which began in the eighteenth century

market forces workings of supply (what is or is not available) and demand (what is or is not wanted)

market rate price that a buyer and seller would agree on if there was no intervention from government

Marxism ideas of Marx and his followers

nationalism active promotion of national interest, often at the expense of humanity as a whole

New Economic Policy (NEP) reintroduction of limited private trading after the Russian Civil War

October Revolution second Russian Revolution of 1917 that brought the communists to power

orthodoxy traditional way of doing things

peasant farm worker or owner of a small farm
personality cult campaign of exaggerated praise for an individual leader
philosopher person who thinks about life
Politburo Soviet cabinet (or small ruling committee elected by the Central Committee)
racism belief that individuals or groups are inferior because they belong to a different race than your own
Red Army army formed by the Bolsheviks to defend their revolution in the civil war
revolutionary in politics, working to overthrow the entire existing order
romanticism philosophy which considers emotion to be more important than thought
socialism set of political ideas that puts more stress on the needs of the community as a whole and less on the short-term wants or needs of the individual
Soviet Russian for "council"
terrorism use of violence to achieve political ends
totalitarian form of society that demands obedience to one set of political, social, and cultural ideas
trade union organization formed to protect and advance the pay and conditions of workers

Index

Afghanistan 40
the arts 32, 53

Berlin Wall 4–5
Bolsheviks 11, 12, 15, 16, 20, 50

Cambodia 11, 35
capitalism 5, 8, 14, 15, 17, 26, 37, 42, 49, 51, 53, 55
Castro, Fidel 45, 49, 54, 59
Chile 12, 50
China 11, 12, 19, 22, 24, 29, 31, 32, 34, 41, 43–5, 48, 54
Cold War 12, 38, 40
collectivization 27–9, 43
Comintern 22, 37
Communes 29
communism and abuses of power 24–5
communism and foreign relations 37–41
communist ideas and ideals 6–10, 18, 38, 42, 45, 52
Communist Party policy 21, 24, 31, 32, 52
Cuba 12, 13, 40, 41, 45, 49, 54
Czechoslovakia/Czech Republic 12, 32, 36, 46, 51

democratic politics 8, 14, 17, 18, 21, 46, 49
Deng Xiaoping 44, 45, 48, 59
developing world 29, 40, 41, 50
dictatorships 17, 22, 23, 52

eastern Europe 12, 13, 19, 32, 38, 42, 54
education 31, 53

French Revolution 6

Germany 4–5, 12, 14, 25, 38
Gorbachev, Mikhail 47, 59
Guevara, Ernesto "Che" 45, 59

Hungary 12, 36, 42, 43

Industrial Revolution 6, 29

Khmer Rouge 35
Khrushchev, Nikita 42, 45
Kim Il Sung 22, 34, 59

labor camps 27
Lenin, Vladimir Ilyich 10, 12, 15, 16, 18, 23, 26, 33, 37, 42, 60
Luxemburg, Rosa 25

Mao Zedong 11, 22, 24, 32, 34, 43, 44, 45, 59–60
market forces 48, 49
Marx, Karl 7–9, 13, 14, 18, 33, 60
Marxist-Leninists 16, 17, 20
media 31, 53

North Korea 12, 19, 22, 34, 40
nuclear weapons 40

peasants 12, 26, 27, 29, 32, 49
personality cult 33, 44, 53
planned economy 26–30, 46, 52

Politburo 21, 22
political police 23–4, 52

religion 33–4
revolutions and takeovers 5, 6, 11–16, 18

shared ownership 6, 9, 26
socialism 6–8, 9, 13, 14, 15, 16, 17, 20, 26, 51
'socialist realism' 32
Soviet Union 5, 11, 12, 13, 15, 17–18, 19, 20, 21–34, 36, 37–41, 42, 51, 54
Stalin, Joseph 12, 22, 23, 24, 27, 33, 38, 42, 60

Tiananmen Square 36, 45
totalitarianism 31, 38
Trotsky, Leon 12, 60

United States 38, 40, 49, 50

Vietnam 11, 19, 24, 40, 41, 49, 54

World War II 12, 38, 39

CABARRUS COUNTY PUBLIC LIBRARY
KANNAPOLIS LIBRARY
KANNAPOLIS, NORTH CAROLINA 28081